Amazing Animal Hunters

Jen Green

amicus

Published by Amicus
P.O. Box 1329, Mankato, Minnesota 56002

Printed in the United States of America at Corporate Graphics, in North Mankato, Minnesota.

Library of Congress Cataloging-in-Publication Data
Green, Jen.
  Bears / Jen Green.
     p. cm. -- (Amazing animal hunters)
  Includes index.
  Summary: "Discusses the life of bears and profiles different types of bears,
  along with providing facts and records on bears"--Provided by publisher.
  ISBN 978-1-60753-044-2 (library binding)
  1. Bears--Juvenile literature. I. Title.
  QL737.C27G7384 2011
  599.78--dc22

                                        2009044218

Created by Q2AMedia
Editor: Katie Dicker
Art Director: Harleen Mehta
Designer: Rohit Juneja
Picture Researcher: Debabrata Sen
Coloring Artists: Aadil Ahmed Siddiqui, Abhijeet Sharma

All words in **bold** can be found in the Glossary on pages 30–31.

Picture credits
t=top b=bottom c=center l=left r=right
Cover images: Novastock Novastock/Photolibrary, Ewan Chesser/Shutterstock

Doug Lindstrand/Photolibrary: Title page, Mario Lopes/Shutterstock: Contents page, Amy & Chuck Wiley/Wales/Photolibrary: 4,
Dani/Jeske/Photolibrary: 5, Corbis/Photolibrary: 6, Photolibrary: 7t, Norbert Rosing/Getty Images: 8, Eric Baccega/Photolibrary: 9,
Upton Photography/Big Stock Photo: 10, Berndt Fischer/Photolibrary: 11, Johnny Johnson/Getty Images: 12, Photogaga/
Dreamstime: 13, Eric Baccega/Nature Picture Library: 14t, Doug Lindstrand/Photolibrary: 15, Steven Kazlowski/Photolibrary: 16,
Fred Bruemmer/Photolibrary: 17t, Patricia Marroquin/Dreamstime: 17b, Jack Milchanowski/Photolibrary: 18, Peter Bisset/
Photolibrary: 19t, Peter Weimann/Photolibrary: 19b, Erwin & Peggy Bauer/Photolibrary: 20, Frank Lukasseck/Photolibrary: 21,
Sue Flood/Getty Images: 22, Steven Kazlowski/Photolibrary: 23, Philippe Henry/Photolibrary: 24, Jan Martin Will/Shutterstock: 25,
Peter J Oxford/Photolibrary: 26, Fenghui/Big Stock Photo: 27t, Keren Su/Corbis: 27b, Susann Parker/Photolibrary: 28, Roland
Mayr/Photolibrary: 29l, Wayne Lawler/Ecoscene: 29r, Photogaga/Photolibrary: 31.

Q2AMedia Art Bank: 7b, 14b.

DAD0043
42010

9 8 7 6 5 4 3 2 1

Contents

Big Brutes

What animal would you least like to meet on a hike in the woods? If you live in North America, you will probably say a bear. Bears are the largest meat-eating animals that live on land. They are incredibly strong and can be bad tempered if disturbed.

Bear Types

Bears are massive **mammals**. They are found on every continent except Africa, Australia, and Antarctica. There are eight **species**, but the best known are polar bears, giant pandas, and brown (grizzly) bears. Two types of black bears live in North America and Asia. There are also three smaller species— sun, sloth, and spectacled bears.

Animals that eat meat are called **carnivores**. Bears eat meat, but they eat plants as well (see page 10).

The grizzly (North American brown bear) is one of the largest, fiercest bears.

Large head

Powerful shoulders

Shaggy fur

Chunky body

Fact or Fiction?

For hundreds of years, people have described bears as slow-witted and lazy because they sleep a lot. A group of bears are called "sloth," which suggests bears are slothful (lazy). It is true that bears spend a lot of time sleeping, but they aren't dim-witted. When awake, they are usually busy looking for their next meal! Many people fear bears for their size and their brute strength.

 Asian black bears have a thick neck and large ears for their size.

GIANT MEAT-EATER

The largest carnivore that ever lived on land was the giant short-faced bear. Twice the size of the biggest modern bear, it stood 6.5 feet (2 m) tall at the shoulder when standing on all fours. This prehistoric giant had very long legs and probably chased antelope on the North American prairies. It died out around 12,500 years ago.

Fur, Teeth, and Claws

Bears are strong, powerful hunters. Their main weapons are their huge clawed paws, which can deliver a shattering, sledgehammer-like blow. When they're on the prowl, their shaggy fur keeps out the cold and wet.

Speed and Disguise

Bears walk on the soles of their feet, as humans do. They usually move on all fours, but they can rear up on their hind legs to threaten an enemy. They can also have a burst of speed to capture their **prey**. Their thick coat keeps them warm and dry. Most bears have brown, black, or reddish fur that blends in with their surroundings. The polar bear's white coat hides it against the Arctic snow.

Strong neck supports the massive head

Shaggy fur can be pale, dark brown, or black

Powerful limbs

A roaring bear is a terrifying sight.

Strength and Weapons

A grizzly bear can weigh more than 1,000 lbs. (450 kg). These heavily-built mammals have strong, stocky limbs and a short, stubby tail. The bear's main strength lies in its massive shoulders and incredibly powerful front limbs. Their long, curving claws can tear open the flesh of an enemy. The long, dagger-like front teeth called canines can be used to seize the bear's prey and to rip meat to shreds.

Keen nose picks up the scent of distant prey

Massive head

Long canine teeth clamp onto struggling prey

Blunt teeth called molars crush plant food

Long, curving claws are used for climbing, digging, and slashing prey

Broad paw has five toes

FUR FACTS

The sloth bear has the shaggiest fur. This Indian bear has very long hair on its shoulders. The sun bear has the shortest fur, to keep it cool in the hot, steamy forests of Southeast Asia.

Bears can kill with one swipe of their enormous paws.

American Black Bears

The black bear is the most common bear in North America. It is smaller than the grizzly, but has the same chunky build, with a large head, strong shoulders, and short limbs. Not all black bears are black—they can be brown or even white!

Tree Climbers

American black bears like to live in forests, but they've also been found in mountains, swamps, fields, and coastal areas. Nimbler than grizzlies, they sometimes climb trees to find food or to escape from danger. They are skillful climbers and can also run fast over short distances.

Ears are small and rounded

Black bear lacks shoulder hump of the grizzly

 Black bears climb trees to find foods such as nuts, berries, and leaves.

Famous Black Bears

Some black bears have become very famous. In 1902, U.S. President Theodore (Teddy) Roosevelt refused to shoot a black bear while on a hunting trip. Soon after, the first "Teddy's bears" appeared in shops and remain popular toys to this day. The writer A.A. Milne based his bear Winnie-the-Pooh on a black bear named Winnipeg, which lived at London Zoo. Smokey the Bear, a symbol for the United States Forest Service, was based on a real black bear **cub** rescued from a forest fire.

SPIRIT BEARS

White-colored black bears are sometimes glimpsed in the misty forests of western North America. They have been called "spirit bears" and are very rare. Years ago, native Americans believed these ghostly bears had supernatural powers. In fact, their pale color results from a rare **trait** called **albinism**.

Ghostly spirit bears are very rare.

Pale-colored fur

Tracking Down Food

Bears are big eaters. They need a lot of food to fuel their huge bulk and are nearly always hungry. Bears have sharp senses when it comes to finding food. They have an amazing knack of turning up wherever there is food present.

Hungry Creatures

Most people think of bears as ferocious meat-eaters, but in fact they are **omnivores**. This means they eat plant foods such as fruits, nuts, and grass, as well as meat. In fact, bears eat just about anything they can get their paws on. Black bears, for example, hunt elk and moose calves, and hook trout and crayfish from rivers. But they also like to eat plants, insects, and honey.

Small ears swivel to catch sounds

Sloth bears eat mainly insects and honey.

Small eyes can only see well up close

Nose can identify many different scents

TOO MUCH TO DRINK

In summer 2004, a black bear was found unconscious near a popular camping spot in Seattle, WA. It had broken into campers' coolers and used its teeth and claws to puncture dozens of beer cans. After drinking the contents, it passed out. The bear was choosy. It drank one type of beer, but ignored another brand after sampling just one can.

Omnivore means "everything-eater." This sun bear is eating an ear of corn.

Super Senses

Bears track down their next meal using their expert senses. Their most important sense is smell. The part of the bear's brain that identifies scents is very well-developed. A polar bear can sniff the scent of a seal up to 20 mi. (32 km) away, for example. Bears have also been known to break into people's cars because they can smell a tasty picnic basket.

The Fearsome Grizzly

Grizzlies are large, ferocious bears. A full-grown grizzly can weigh as much as a young elephant and is strong enough to kill a stag. Grizzlies are famous for being aggressive and bad-tempered, but they have a gentle side, too.

Armed and Dangerous

In North America, brown bears are called grizzlies. The name comes from the bear's silver-tipped fur, which looks grey and "grizzled" (streaked with gray hair). If surprised, these enormous bears will rear up on their back legs, roar loudly, and bare their teeth in a ferocious snarl. Some grizzlies have attacked humans because they feel threatened. The most dangerous grizzlies are usually the mothers who are protecting their cubs. Grizzlies can be grouchy with one another, but usually get along when there is lots of food around.

A cornered bear may charge its enemy at high speed. Once these bears start running, they are not very good at stopping!

Sharp canine teeth hold slippery fish tight in the bear's jaws

A fishing bear waits by a waterfall. When a salmon leaps up, the grizzly is waiting with open jaws!

Seasonal Feast

Like black bears, grizzlies are not fussy with their food. They will prey on mammals as large as seals, deer, and moose. Down at the beach, they hunt crabs and crayfish by overturning pebbles. They will also scavenge stinking meat from the bodies of dead whales. The grizzly's diet changes with the seasons. In spring, these bears feed on tender shoots. In summer, they wade into rivers to feast on salmon that have swum upstream to spawn (produce eggs). In autumn, they gorge themselves on nuts, fruits, and berries as they prepare for their winter sleep.

PLAYING DEAD

In 2008, a Canadian man, Brent Case, survived a grizzly bear attack by pretending to be dead. As the bear attacked, Case dropped to the ground and didn't react even when the bear began to gnaw his scalp! Finally, the bear lost interest. Case ran to his car and fled in search of help.

Home, Sweet Home

Bears live mainly in the northern **hemisphere**. The brown bear is the most common. It lives in North America, parts of Europe, the Middle East, and across Asia. In contrast, the giant panda is only found in the bamboo forests of central China.

Where Do Bears Live?

Bears can survive in many different climates—from hot, **tropical** regions to the icy Arctic. Many bears live in forests. Sun, sloth, and spectacled bears are expert tree climbers that live in warm climates. They use their sharp claws for climbing and to strip back the bark as they search for insects. Spectacled bears and giant pandas have patchy markings that blend in with the trees and leaves.

The dark coloring of the spectacled bear helps it to hide in the forest.

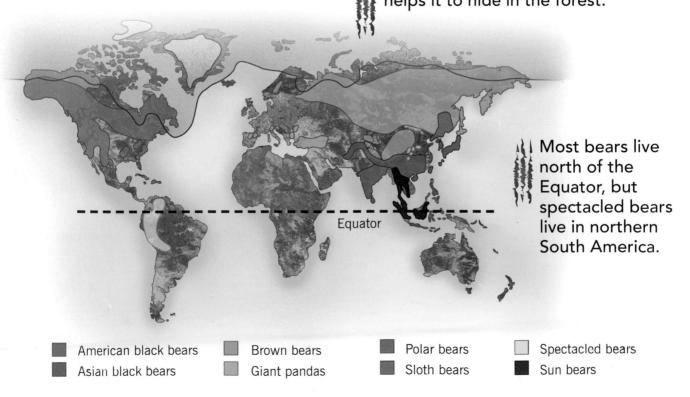

Equator

Most bears live north of the Equator, but spectacled bears live in northern South America.

- ■ American black bears
- ■ Asian black bears
- ■ Brown bears
- ■ Giant pandas
- ■ Polar bears
- ■ Sloth bears
- ■ Spectacled bears
- ■ Sun bears

No Trespassing

Many bears travel long distances to find food. Each animal has a **home range**—the area in which it lives and hunts. Brown and black bear **territories** vary from just a small patch to a huge area covering 193 square miles (500 sq km). Some bears, especially females, fiercely defend their territories to keep out intruders. Each bear marks its territory by leaving scents and clawing trees to show that this particular patch is taken. Trespassers beware!

FINDING THE WAY

Bears have an amazing sense of direction. This helps them to find their way as they wander about their territory. Bears also recognize natural landmarks such as rivers, routes through the mountains, or a favorite berry-bearing tree.

The size of a bear's territory depends on how much food there is. Territories are small where there is plenty of food.

The Ice Bear

The polar bear lives in one of the harshest places on Earth—the Arctic. The top predator of its icy world, it lives by hunting seals. This is the only bear that survives on a mostly meat diet—and the only bear to see humans as strictly prey.

All at Sea

Polar bears live and hunt on the ice-covered Arctic Ocean. They can dive off floating ice into the chilly waters. They spend a lot of time in the sea and are expert swimmers. They use their front paws to swim doggy-paddle, and can keep up a steady pace of 6 mph (10 km/h) for hours. Polar bears have been seen swimming 100 miles (160 km) from land. Dense fur and a thick layer of **blubber** keep the bear warm in the icy water, where a human would die in a matter of minutes.

A bear's coat has two layers—long outer hairs to repel water and dense, woolly underfur for warmth

The polar bear's small head and long neck create a smooth shape for efficient swimming.

Catching Seals

Polar bears mostly prey on seals, which hunt fish under the sea ice. An adult seal will keep a polar bear well-fed for at least a week. A bear may sneak up on a seal, inching closer on its belly and keeping very still whenever the seal looks up. When the seal is within range, it charges at top speed. Or it may wait patiently by a seal's breathing hole, for hours if necessary. When a seal pops up for air, the bear clubs it with its paw or grabs it in its jaws.

A bear waits by a seal's breathing hole. Seals use these holes to gulp air between dives.

Pointed canine teeth sink into rubbery seal flesh

Polar bears have special scissor-shaped teeth, called carnassials, at the back of their jaws. They use these to slice through flesh.

Winter Sleep

Bears that live in cold places survive winter in a deep sleep called **hibernation**. It makes sense to sleep to save energy when food is scarce. Most polar bears don't hibernate despite the harsh Arctic winter. But female polar bears hibernate when they are pregnant to save energy for the birth of their cubs.

Getting Ready

Bears prepare for hibernation by feasting in the autumn. They eat as much rich food as possible to put on weight. A thick layer of fat will give their body the energy it needs during hibernation. As winter arrives, the bear retires to its **den**. This could be a cave, a rotten tree, or a hollow in the ground dug with the bear's sharp claws. Bears have also been known to hibernate under log cabins or beneath road bridges.

Bears gorge on rich food such as berries in autumn. At the start of winter, some bears are very fat!

Slowing Down

Bears don't eat or drink during hibernation. Their heartbeat gets slower and their body temperature may drop by several degrees. The bear actually looks dead—but it can still wake up quite quickly if danger threatens. When spring arrives, the bear wakes up and goes out hunting. It will have lost up to half its body weight over the winter months, so it will be very hungry indeed!

This black bear may have spent up to six months in its winter den.

A brown bear shows her cub the world for the first time, in spring.

Raising Cubs

Most bears like to live alone, but males and females come together in the breeding season. If two male bears meet at this time, they will fight for the chance to mate with a female. Male polar bears may fight to the death. The winner may even eat the loser!

Newborn Cubs

Black and brown bears mate in summer. Up to four tiny cubs are born in the den six to nine months later. Newborn black and brown bears weigh under 11 oz (300 g) and are the size of rats. Unlike polar bear cubs, they have no fur. Their eyes are tightly shut and they are very helpless. They remain in the den for about four months, until they are strong enough to explore the outside world.

Male bears fight ferociously to be able to mate with a female.

Leaving the Den

In May or June, brown and black bear cubs leave the den for the first time. They stay close to their mother and still drink her milk. Female bears are fiercely protective and will defend their cubs against predators. Mothers show their cubs where to find food and how to hunt tricky prey such as seals. At about three years old, the cubs are old enough to take care of themselves. They leave the mother and wander off to find a territory of their own.

Newborn cubs drink their mother's milk. They begin to eat berries at about six months old.

CANNIBAL BEARS

Male bears are a major threat to bear cubs. Polar, black, and grizzly males may view a cub as a tasty snack. If a mother and her young are threatened by a male grizzly, the female will urge her cubs up a tree. She knows the grizzly is too heavy to follow.

Beware of the Bear

Bears are powerful, unpredictable creatures and many people are rightly scared of them. But bears are also very popular. In books and movies, they are often shown as cuddly, gentle creatures. The reality is very different—real bears can be a menace.

Bears and People

Disney's *The Jungle Book* features a bear named Baloo. Baloo is friendly and sociable. He takes care of a human boy, Mowgli. Real bears aren't friendly. They are usually just as wary of us as we are of them. Sometimes, hungry bears are attracted to towns by the smell of food. They scavenge for scraps in city dumps and trash cans. These bears become a nuisance.

This bear is stealing scraps from a city dump.

Safety First

Brown, black, and polar bears have been known to attack humans. Between 1900 and 2003, bears in North America killed more than 50 people. Many of these attacks took place in the countryside when bears were surprised by people and lashed out because they felt threatened. If you live in or visit bear country, there are a few rules to follow. Never feed bears or leave food where bears can reach it. If you see a bear, give it plenty of space and never approach a female and her cubs. When hiking through a forest, make a noise to warn any bears that you are coming.

POLAR BEAR TROUBLE

The town of Churchill, on Canada's Hudson Bay, is known as the polar bear capital. In autumn, hungry bears arrive to scavenge from the town's garbage dumps. Some bears are drugged by a vet and transported out of town, but find their way back again. Others are kept in a special "jail" until the bay freezes over and they can safely be released into the wild.

Never feed bears, even from a car. Bears have been known to break into cars to steal food.

Bears in Danger

As top predators, bears only have one real enemy —humans. For centuries, bears have been hunted and people have also taken over the wild places where they live. The result is that many types of bears are now scarce.

Hunting and Clearing

For hundreds of years, people have killed bears for their thick fur and stringy meat. Body parts such as gall bladders are used in Chinese medicine. Farmers and ranchers kill bears because they break in to eat crops or **livestock**. In Canada and parts of the United States, grizzly bears are still shot for sport. Over the last century, huge areas of forest and other **habitats** have been cleared for timber, or to make room for new farmland, roads, and towns. Bears are threatened when they lose their habitat because food becomes scarce.

People shoot bears for sport, or because they are frightened of them.

Saving Bears

Of the eight species of bears, only brown and American black bears are still found in quite large numbers, and even they are less widespread than they used to be. Many people are now working hard to save bears from **extinction**. This type of work is called **conservation**. The hunting of rare bear species is banned in most countries. Threatened bears are sometimes bred in **captivity**, and their young are released into the wild. The best way of saving bears is to preserve whole habitats by creating national parks and other protected areas.

POLAR BEARS AT RISK

For centuries, polar bears have been hunted for their fur and meat. Now they face a new danger—**global warming**. World temperatures are getting warmer, and the Arctic ice is melting. The bears are losing their habitat and their hunting grounds.

Polar bears hunt seals on the sea ice. As temperatures on Earth rise, their hunting grounds are melting.

The Giant Panda

Giant pandas are unusual bears. While most bears eat a variety of plant and animal food, pandas eat mainly one plant, bamboo. They bark or bleat instead of roar and don't hibernate even in the coldest winters.

Bamboo-Eater

The giant panda lives in remote forests in China. Its distinctive black and white coat blends in with the dappled forest, particularly after snow has fallen. Pandas mainly eat bamboo—a tough, stringy food that is hard to digest and not very nourishing. Pandas spend up to 12 hours a day eating just to get enough nutrients from their food. The panda has been hunted for its fur and meat. It is now the world's rarest bear.

Pandas eat bamboo shoots in spring, leaves in summer and autumn, and stems in winter.

Help for Pandas

With their cuddly looks, pandas are very appealing. They have become an international symbol for conservation and people are working hard to save them. About half of the forests where pandas live are now protected. Killing a panda is a very serious crime in China—punishable by death! Pandas have been bred in zoos and nature reserves since the 1960s. However, young pandas rarely thrive in zoos, and there is not enough wild habitat left for them to be released into the wild.

These baby pandas are being well-looked after in a zoo.

EXTRA THUMBS

Pandas have six "fingers" on each hand! A very long wrist bone sticks out to form an extra thumb on each paw. Pandas use these false thumbs, and their real thumbs, to grasp bamboo while feeding.

Pandas use their false thumbs to hold bamboo stems.

Facts and Records

Bears are the largest, fiercest meat-eaters around on land today. They are amazing in many ways.

Kodiak bears are heavyweights among grizzlies.

Largest and Smallest

- The world's largest bears are polar bears and brown Kodiak bears.

- Male polar bears can measure up to 10 ft. (3 m) long, and weigh 1,500 lbs. (680 kg)—as much as eight human adults. Female polar bears are up to 50 percent smaller than the males.

- Kodiak bears are grizzlies from Alaska. They measure up to 9 ft. (2.7 m) long and can weigh 1,700 lbs. (770 kg). They grow very large and heavy on a rich diet high in salmon.

- The sun bear is the smallest bear. It only measures up to 4.6 ft. (1.4 m) long, with a top weight of 143 lbs. (65 kg).

Did You Know?

- Grizzly bears can run as fast as a horse.

- Bamboo makes up 99 percent of the panda's diet. The remainder includes insects on the bamboo and dead meat that they find.

- In winter, instead of hibernating, polar bears use the frozen sea ice to explore more of their hunting grounds.

Body Facts

- A bear's sense of smell is around 100 times greater than a human's.

- The giant panda has a large head for its body. This may be because it needs a strong jaw and neck muscles to chomp on bamboo.

Names and Numbers

- A male bear is called a "boar" and a female bear is called a "sow."

- Sun bears are named after the bright patch of fur on their chests. They are also called honey bears because they eat honey.

- Bears live for 20–30 years in the wild. One captive brown bear survived to the age of 47.

A full-grown male polar bear can be more than 10 ft. (3 m) tall when it stands on its hind legs.

Record-Breakers

- Polar bears have the largest home ranges of any bear. The area in which they hunt can be as big as the state of Maine!

- Sun bears have the longest claws of any bear, and also the longest tongues. They use their curving claws to climb trees, searching for insects and honey, which they lick up with their 9.8-inch (25-cm) tongue.

Glossary

albinism
a condition in which a person or animal does not have any natural coloring in the skin, hair, or eyes

blubber
a layer of fat below the skin

captivity
when an animal is kept in a zoo or wildlife park

carnivore
an animal that eats meat

conservation
the protection of natural habitats, plants, and animals

den
an animal's home

extinction
no longer in existence, having died out

global warming
a steady rise in the Earth's temperature, partly caused by burning fossil fuels such as coal, oil, and gas

habitat
a particular place where plants and animals live, such as a tropical forest or desert

hemisphere
one of the two halves of the world, as divided by the Equator

hibernation
a deep sleep that allows animals to survive the cold of winter

home range
the whole area in which an animal lives and looks for food

livestock
animals that are kept by people or farmers to eat or to sell

mammal
an animal that feeds its young milk and has hair on its body

omnivore
an animal that eats plants and meat

predator
an animal that hunts others for food

prey
an animal that is eaten for food by another

species
a particular type of animal, such as a grizzly bear

territory
an area where an animal lives, hunts, and breeds, and which it may defend against others of its kind

trait
a feature or characteristic

tropical
an area or climate that is warm and often wet, close to the equator (the imaginary line around the Earth's middle)

Index

Web Finder

American Bear Association
www.americanbear.org
Facts and figures about bears from a bear reserve in Minnesota.

National Geographic
http://animals.nationalgeographic.com
Search this site to learn more about grizzly, black, and polar bears.

North American Bear Center
www.bear.org/website
Learn all about bears, with video links showing real bears in action!

Polar Bears International
www.polarbearsinternational.org/bear-facts
A site dedicated to polar bears.

WWF—Local to Global Environmental Conservation
www.panda.org
Find out about bears at risk from this conservation organization
whose symbol is the giant panda.